ASSERT YOURSELF

BULLET GUIDE

Hodder Education, 338 Euston Road, London NW1 3BH

Hodder Education is an Hachette UK company

First published in UK 2012 by Hodder Education

This edition published 2012

Copyright © 2012 Steve Bavister and Amanda Vickers

The moral rights of the author have been asserted.

Database right Hodder Education (makers)

Artworks (internal and cover): Peter Lubach
Cover concept design: Two Associates

Also available in ebook

All rights reserved. No part of this publication may be reproduced, stored in a retrieval system or transmitted in any form or by any means, electronic, mechanical, photocopying, recording or otherwise, without the prior permission in writing of Hodder Education, or as expressly permitted by law, or under terms agreed with the appropriate reprographic rights organization. Enquiries concerning reproduction outside the scope of the above should be sent to the Rights Department, Hodder Education, at the address above.

You must not circulate this book in any other binding or cover and you must impose this same condition on any acquirer.

British Library Cataloguing in Publication Data: a catalogue record for this title is available from the British Library.

10 9 8 7 6 5 4 3 2 1

The publisher has used its best endeavours to ensure that any website addresses referred to in this book are correct and active at the time of going to press. However, the publisher and the author have no responsibility for the websites and can make no guarantee that a site will remain live or that the content will remain relevant, decent or appropriate.

The publisher has made every effort to mark as such all words which it believes to be trademarks. The publisher should also like to make it clear that the presence of a word in the book, whether marked or unmarked, in no way affects its legal status as a trademark.

Every reasonable effort has been made by the publisher to trace the copyright holders of material in this book. Any errors or omissions should be notified in writing to the publisher, who will endeavour to rectify the situation for any reprints and future editions.

Hachette UK's policy is to use papers that are natural, renewable and recyclable products and made from wood grown in sustainable forests. The logging and manufacturing processes are expected to conform to the environmental regulations of the country of origin.

www.hoddereducation.co.uk

Typeset by Stephen Rowling/Springworks

Printed in Spain

Durham County Council Libraries, Learning and Culture

C0 1 71 17403 8B
Askews & Holts
158.2

ASSERT YOURSELF
BULLET GUIDE

Steve Bavister and Amanda Vickers

About the authors

Amanda Vickers and Steve Bavister are directors of Speak First, a fast-growing global training and coaching consultancy that specializes in communication skills – including personal impact, managing the media, presentation skills, influencing, coaching and mentoring skills. They are experts in business communication and deliver training and coaching around the world for a wide range of organizations.

Before joining Speak First, Amanda worked for a global bank, both within the business and ultimately in a senior learning and development role, in which she successfully managed a team of 60 people. Steve worked at a senior level for an international media company, where he was responsible for a staff of 80.

Steve and Amanda have Honours degrees in Psychology and are Master Practitioners of Neuro Linguistic Programming (NLP), which gives them a rich understanding of what makes people tick. Together they have written a number of books, including *Essential NLP*, *Confident Coaching*, *Present with Impact and Confidence* and *Personal Impact*.

Contents

1	Understanding assertiveness	1
2	The origins of aggressive behaviour	13
3	Assertive body language	25
4	The voice of assertiveness	37
5	Power talk – the language of assertiveness	49
6	Saying what you think, feel and want	61
7	Pushing back and saying 'no'	73
8	Feedback and criticism	85
9	Assertiveness in challenging situations	97
10	Moving to being more assertive	109

Introduction

One of the most valuable and liberating skills you can acquire in life is assertiveness. Most people are non-assertive or aggressive at times, and it is much more effective to be assertive. All too often many of us don't express our feelings, opinions, wants and needs as assertively as we might. The language we use is weak rather than powerful. When our voice becomes loud or harsh in tone it signals aggression. A quiet voice and soft tone indicates non-assertive behaviour. When someone is assertive they appear and sound confident – people listen to their opinions.

Saying what you think, want and feel is the key to assertiveness. When you're assertive you make requests, state your opinions, disagree when you want to and say 'no' to others rather than ending up doing what you don't want to do. Another skill that requires assertiveness to be effective is giving and receiving feedback. Many people don't enjoy giving or receiving negative feedback and some people don't mind it at all. They experience it as something useful rather than perceiving it as an attack. It is easy to develop the skills for giving feedback and attitude for receiving it once you know how.

Some people find it easy to be assertive in everyday situations but struggle when faced with difficult people or in specific environments. They fear that, if they become more assertive, people won't like them. Instead of saying what they think, they either avoid the situation or accommodate other people's needs at their own expense. Tough situations are when your assertiveness skills are needed most. Follow the advice, tips and techniques in this book and you will find it's easier than you think to become assertive without going over the top.

1 Understanding assertiveness

You'll learn many skills in your lifetime, and **one of the most valuable and important** is assertiveness. Wherever you go, whatever you do, you'll communicate with people and build relationships. **To be able to do this effectively you need to be assertive**. And the first step to mastery is to understand what assertiveness is and what it isn't.

Most people can identify non-assertive behaviour when they experience it in others. They are also often confused about the difference between assertive and aggressive behaviour. Read on to make sure you're on the right track.

This chapter will help you to:

* understand why lack of assertiveness is a problem
* recognize the range of situations in which assertiveness can be applied
* appreciate the differences among assertive, non-assertive and aggressive behaviour
* understand how the life position adopted in childhood affects our behaviour
* be aware of your rights and responsibilities in communicating assertively.

The only healthy communication style is assertive communication.

Jim Rohn

Why lack of assertiveness is a problem

Many people lack assertiveness. They find it hard to **ask for what they want**, **express their feelings** honestly, **say 'no' to others** and put forward their opinions. A lack of assertiveness holds them back – both in their careers and in their personal lives.

Seven benefits of being assertive

1. Feel **more comfortable** in a range of social situations.
2. Know how to say no to others.
3. Be **more confident** to speak up in different situations.
4. Be better able to give honest feedback.
5. Feel equipped to deal with senior or difficult people.
6. Be **able to influence** people more effectively.
7. Get more of **what you want** in life.

When and with whom do you want to be assertive?

Everyone, everywhere! In group situations, one to one, with colleagues at work, with friends and family.

Common situations in which you need to have assertive skills and behaviour include:

* making requests
* refusing requests – saying 'no'
* following up on requests
* saying what you think and feel
* standing by your opinion
* challenging the opinions of others
* disagreeing with someone
* giving negative feedback
* receiving negative feedback
* giving praise
* receiving praise
* delivering bad news.

There's a lot of confusion out there!

The big problem with assertiveness is that **people think that they know what it is** – and **many are wrong**. They **think that it means being forceful, confrontational and 'in your face'** – saying what you think 'no matter what'. But that's not assertiveness – that's aggression.

If you want to learn how to be assertive, it's important to understand what it really is.

The assertiveness zone

There is a continuum, with non-assertive at one end, aggressive at the other and assertiveness in the middle. **Assertive behaviour varies between quietly, firmly and strongly assertive.** You will be most effective when you're **within the assertiveness zone** and move between the quietly/firmly/strongly according to the situation.

Non-assertive	Assertive	Aggressive
	Assertiveness zone	
Quietly	Firmly	Strongly

The basic difference between being assertive and being aggressive is how our words and behaviour affect the rights and well-being of others.

Sharon Anthony Bower

Definitions

In their seminal book *Assertiveness at Work* Ken and Kate Back define assertiveness, aggression and non-assertiveness in the following ways.

Assertiveness

'Standing up for your own rights in such a way that you don't violate another person's rights. Expressing your needs, wants, opinions, feelings and beliefs in direct, honest and appropriate ways.'

Aggression

'Standing up for your own rights, in a way that violates the rights of others. Ignoring or dismissing the needs, wants, opinions, feelings and beliefs of other people.'

Non-assertiveness

'Failing to stand up for your rights, in a way that others can easily disregard them. Expressing your needs, wants, opinions, feelings and beliefs in apologetic, diffident or self-effacing ways. Failing to express your needs, wants, opinions, feelings and beliefs.'

Forms of non-assertiveness

Accommodating
When you accommodate you give up on what's important to you in order to maintain a relationship with someone else.

Avoiding
When you avoid you give up what's important to you and avoid discussing it with the person.

What about passive–aggressive behaviour?
Passive–aggressive behaviour takes the form of **covert aggression**. A person **behaving in this way** doesn't **directly confront** the other person. Such behaviour includes **silence, not taking action** and even **sabotage**. When asked if there's a problem he or she will **say 'no'** – but **doesn't mean it.**

What's your life position?

In his popular book *I'm OK – You're Not OK* Thomas Harris argues that human beings adopt **one of four life positions**, based largely on their early childhood experiences.

People in quadrant 1 realize that they and others are of **equal importance** and behave accordingly.

	You're OK	You're not OK
I'm OK	1 Assertive win–win	2 Aggressive win–lose
I'm not OK	3 Non-assertive lose–win	4 Passive–aggressive lose–lose

Those in quadrant 2 **prioritize their own wants and needs** over the wants and needs of others.

People in quadrant 3 put **others' needs above their own**, which leads to non-assertive behaviour.

Those in quadrant 4 see neither themselves nor others as being important or of value.

Bullet Guide: Assert Yourself

Know your rights and responsibilities

Understanding your rights and the responsibilities you have to others is central to being assertive.

Rights	Responsibilities
To be **treated with respect** – as an intelligent, capable and equal human being	To treat others with respect – as intelligent, capable and equal human beings
To state my needs, feelings and opinions and to **ask for what I want**	To allow others to express their needs, feelings and opinions and to ask for what they want
To **change my mind** without offering reasons	To allow others to change their minds
To **ask for more time** or information	To listen when others ask for more time or information
To say yes or no without feeling guilty	To take responsibility for the consequences of my actions

2 The origins of aggressive behaviour

Why do some people become aggressive while others shrink from conflict? Is it nature, or is it nurture? Are we born to be wild, or do we learn to be mild? The evidence is compelling and conclusive. Most of us demonstrate aggressive behaviour when we're younger and then learn to control our impulses as part of the socialization process.

Understanding where aggression comes from and how the beliefs we hold drive our behaviour helps us to shift to using assertive rather than aggressive behaviour more often.

This chapter will help you to:

* understand where aggression comes from
* appreciate why people behave the way they do
* recognize that the 'rules' we live by drive our behaviour
* know how to change these rules to achieve better results
* manage the emotions that lead to aggressive behaviour
* know what to do when others behave aggressively.

> **Peace cannot be kept by force; it can only be achieved by understanding.**
>
> Albert Einstein

Nature or nurture?

Many children are **naturally aggressive**. Research has shown this definitively. **One in every four interactions** between children aged 2–4 has an **aggressive element**: pushing someone, grabbing a toy, pulling hair and sometimes even biting.

Why do we do this? Because at this age our brain isn't fully developed and we have **little control over our impulses**. When we want something we **want it now** – and we don't really understand the concept of sharing and co-operating.

We are also programmed by our genes to vie for the **top spot in the pecking order**, and at this age a display of aggression is the easiest way to achieve it.

The biology of non-assertion and aggression

Why, when **behaving assertively usually leads to the best outcome**, do so many people behave aggressively or non-assertively? Much of it is down to biology.

Dig behind our sophisticated 21st-century human brain and you soon discover that we have another brain that is **200,000 years old**. This reacts to perceived threats via the well-known **fight or flight response**:

1 First we 'freeze' – we stop moving and breathing while we take stock of the situation.
2 If we think that the other person is more powerful than us, we 'take flight', or, if we can't, we accommodate and acquiesce: a non-assertive response.
3 If we think that we're in the stronger position we 'fight' – we prepare for action and behave in a forceful and aggressive manner.

Rules we live by

Feelings aren't random. They don't exist in a vacuum – they are always **the result of thinking.** We all have rules we live by – **beliefs, values and norms that drive our actions** – and this is true of assertiveness. Many of these rules operate out of conscious awareness and take the form of:

- shoulds/shouldn'ts
- musts/mustn'ts
- cans/can'ts
- right/wrong
- good/bad.

Typical rules that non-assertive people often follow are:

- I must always be nice to others.
- It's wrong to hurt other people's feelings.
- I could never tell my boss exactly what I think.
- People should never brag about their achievements.

Where feelings and behaviours come from

Thoughts → Feelings → Actions

Example

When we believe we must never be forceful in our dealings with others, we will behave non-assertively for fear of coming across too strong.

Ask yourself

Where did your rules come from? If you're like most people, you learned them in childhood. **Parents shape the attitudes of their children** by rewarding behaviours they like and punishing behaviours they don't like. They learn what's 'right' and 'wrong', what's 'good' and 'bad' and what they 'should' and 'must' do.

Assertiveness is not what you do, it's who you are.

Shakti Gawain

Disputing and debating

Just because you have a thought in your head **doesn't make it true**. People believe all sorts of things that **don't stand scrutiny** in the cold light of day. When you examine them, you realize that they **don't make any sense**.

What if you were to **debate and dispute** some of the rules you have about assertiveness – and then change them? When you change the rules you change your behaviour – and that can lead to you **getting the outcome you want**.

Bullet Guide: Assert Yourself

Example 1

Rule 'I must always be nice to others.'

Resulting behaviour Not saying what you think and feel.

Dispute 'Always'?

New rule 'I will be nice to people whenever possible, but sometimes I will need to be firm with them.'

New behaviour Saying what you think and feel.

Example 2

Rule 'People should never brag about their achievements.'

Resulting behaviour Finding it hard/impossible to say positive things about yourself.

Dispute Saying positive things about yourself – for example giving a 'good news update' – isn't bragging.

New rule 'I will say positive things about myself, but I will keep it factual, and not over-egg it.'

New behaviour Finding a way of raising your profile internally and externally.

Why do some people behave aggressively?

Most people learn to **control their aggressive urges** as part of the socialization process as they grow up – but **not all do**. Some end up with a 'short fuse' or even an anger management issue.

When an **important value gets violated** (e.g. 'People should respect others') they become aggressive, sometimes even shouting and screaming because they're so angry and frustrated. Their **amygdala** – the brain's emotional centre – has been **hijacked**, and they're no longer thinking rationally. This leads to aggressive behaviour, which can sometimes, at its most extreme, be physical in nature.

How to manage your own aggression

1. **Recognize your patterns** Be aware of the kinds of situations and people that lead you to behave in an aggressive manner.
2. **Notice warning signals** Be aware of when you're starting to get frustrated, upset or annoyed.
3. **Interrupt the pattern** Do something that stops you being aggressive: take a deep breath, think about something different.
4. **Get out of the situation** If you find yourself getting aggressive, take a few minutes to calm down.

How to manage other people's aggression

1. **Be aware of others' patterns** Recognize the situations and triggers that lead to aggressive behaviour in people you know well – and take action.
2. **Notice warning signals** Be aware of when others are starting to get frustrated, upset or annoyed.
3. **Interrupt the pattern** Do or say something that stops them becoming aggressive.
4. **Get out of the situation** If you think it's likely they're going to get aggressive, take time out or walk away.

3 Assertive body language

Can you tell whether someone's assertive just by looking at them? Mostly you can. There are many ways in which **a person's body shows that they're comfortable and confident** – or if they're anxious and nervous. Aggressive body language is easy to observe in others – you can see the tension! Even small changes can be all too evident to other people. Learning **the secrets of how to stand, move, gesture and make eye contact** will ensure that others experience you as assertive.

This chapter will help you to:

- appreciate the importance of body language in assertiveness
- know how to get your posture and stance right
- understand how to make powerful eye contact
- use 'dominance' gestures to maximize your impact.

If you don't stand for something, you'll fall for anything.

Malcolm X

Why body language is so important

Communication happens on **multiple levels** across three channels:

- verbal (what you say)
- vocal (how you say it)
- visual (what others see).

Much of the impact we make on others comes from the visual channel – **how we stand or sit, move and gesture as well as our facial expressions and eye contact**. In fact, when there's a mismatch among the visual, vocal and verbal channels, people almost always believe the visual over the vocal and the vocal over the verbal.

The 'silent messages' you're constantly 'beaming' into the world reveal how you feel, and **if you appear nervous** or uncomfortable (see overleaf) **you'll come across as non-assertive**.

It's crucial you create a strong first impression, because first impressions are lasting impressions. That means **ensuring that your body language comes across as confident** and assertive.

Assertively making eye contact

Eye contact is one of the most immediate ways of demonstrating your assertiveness. **When you look people in the eye you come across as trustworthy**. When your eye contact is poor, others may consider you shifty or timid. But if your eye contact is too strong, you'll be thought too forceful:

Do	Don't
✔ Look others directly in the eye.	✘ Gaze above the eyes or to the side.
✔ Hold contact long enough to get a real sense of connection.	✘ Just glance at the other person.
	✘ Look for more than 2 seconds.
✔ Keep your head upright.	✘ Tip your head down.
✔ Smile with your eyes.	✘ Stare intently.

Basic human contact – the meeting of eyes, the exchanging of words – is to the psyche what oxygen is to the brain.

Martha Beck

Standing tall

The military. Finishing schools. The police. They all train people to **stand tall, with shoulders back and chest out.** Why? Because it looks assertive.

Tall people are perceived to be more confident and more intelligent than shorter people – and there is evidence to suggest that they earn more. Don't lower your apparent height by slumping, with your shoulders rounded. Stand tall and others will immediately **perceive you to be assertive.**

Sitting up assertively

Three ways of looking assertive when sitting down:

1. **Sit close to the table** – pull the chair in tight so your belly is no more than 15 cm from the table.
2. **Lean forward slightly** – this shows engagement and instantly makes you more assertive.
3. **Rest your lower arms and hands on the table** – you want to be able to gesture for maximum impact.

Three things to avoid when sitting down:

1. **Don't collapse your body inwards** – you look as if you're protecting yourself and being defensive.
2. **Never lean back and stretch out** – it makes you appear, at best, uninterested and, at worst, aggressive.
3. **Don't rest your hands in your lap** – it can seem as if you're trying to hide them.

Hands and gestures

One of the most powerful ways of conveying assertiveness through body language is by using your hands. So don't stand or sit there like a statue, use some of the following dynamic gestures:

- **The chop**: a short, sharp, downward movement of one hand for emphasis.

- **Fist to the table:** gently and firmly tap the table with your fist to emphasize a point.

- **Knuckles**: push your knuckles forward with palms towards you to convey confidence.

- Any **straight-wristed gesture** looks stronger and more assertive than a limp, wishy-washy one.

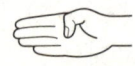

Face the facts

People pay more attention to your face than any other part of your body, so you need to make sure you're **sending out the right message**.

TOP TIPS

Smile! A smile says you're happy, confident, approachable and a whole lot more.

Make it a natural smile Let your eyes light up and your crow's feet crinkle.

But don't smile too much It looks as if you're too eager to please others.

Keep your face neutral and warm Other expressions often convey non-assertive/aggressive nuances.

Avoid frowning (as if you're worried) It looks as if you're uncertain about the response you'll get.

Assertively shaking hands

1. **Make sure your hands are dry** – no one likes a sweaty handshake.
2. **Grasp the other person's hand firmly** – avoid a weak, dead fish or a fierce crusher handshake.
3. **Make sure you go 'web to web'** – don't just grab the fingers.
4. **Give it a couple of pumps straight up and down** – any less feels insincere, any more is overfriendly.
5. **Avoid using two hands** – bringing a second into play can make you seem like a second-rate politician.

CASE STUDY

Simon came across as fairly assertive, but **his handshake was weak** – and it affected him negatively to a surprising degree. People thought **he might be as weak as his handshake**, and were reluctant to trust him.

Bullet Guide: Assert Yourself

Avoiding signs of discomfort

Assertiveness gets compromised **whenever you show signs of discomfort** and nervousness, because you **appear to lack confidence** – and confidence is at the heart of assertiveness. So avoid the following:

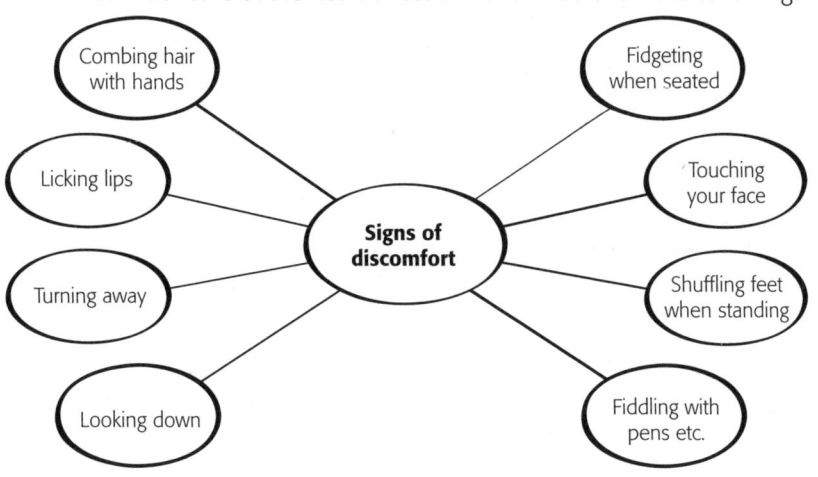

Signs of discomfort
- Combing hair with hands
- Licking lips
- Turning away
- Looking down
- Fidgeting when seated
- Touching your face
- Shuffling feet when standing
- Fiddling with pens etc.

4 The voice of assertiveness

Close your eyes and **listen intently to someone's voice**, and **you can tell more or less immediately how assertive** they are. Nothing else gives the game away as quickly. A full-on voice signals aggression. A quiet voice and soft tone indicate non-assertiveness. So much of the meaning we make of communication comes directly from the voice, and it's easy to get this wrong. If you **want people to take note of what you say** – and do what you ask – you need to **make sure that your voice is assertive**.

This chapter will help you to:

* understand why the voice plays a vital role in assertive communication
* adjust the volume of your voice so that it sounds assertive
* recognize why it's sometimes useful to use a command inflexion
* appreciate how hesitancy leads to non-assertive communication
* avoid fillers such as ums and ers
* change an aggressive voice into an assertive one.

> **Words mean more than what is set down on paper. It takes the human voice to infuse them with deeper meaning.**
>
> Maya Angelou

Why is an assertive voice vital to success?

1 When there's a mismatch between the words you say and the way you say them people will **give more weight to the vocal element**.
2 When your voice is **quiet and soft**, others may think you're **timid and lack confidence**.
3 It's **easier to get people's attention** in groups or meetings with an assertive voice that commands attention.
4 People **take your message more seriously** when you articulate clearly and your voice is assertive.

CASE STUDY

The easy chatter dissipated when James kicked off the meeting in a firm, confident tone. Jo chipped in with a cost-saving idea, but her voice was soft and hesitant, and nobody responded to what she said. The discussion moved on to the next point.

Speak up!

An assertive voice is **neither too loud nor too quiet**. Many people are surprised when they hear a recording of their voice to find it sounds a lot quieter (or sometimes louder) than they imagined.

When your voice is quiet people are likely to perceive you as non-assertive. It gives the impression that you lack confidence or belief in what you want to convey.

How do you rate your volume?

| 1 | 3 | 7 | 10 |

Non-assertive | Assertive | Aggressive

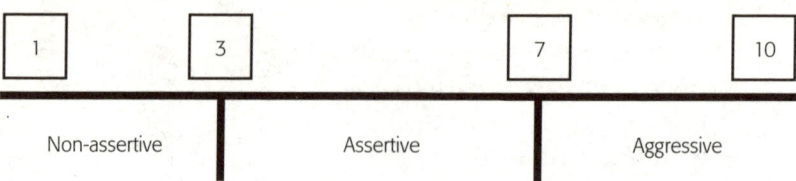

Ask some people you trust to **rate the volume of your voice** on a scale of 1 to 10, where 1 is a whisper and 10 is shouting. If you're rated less than 5 you may have a problem. While 3–4 is quietly assertive, those who speak louder may consider you weak. **Speaking at '6' conveys assertiveness** but without any 'edge'. Beyond 7 you will start to be perceived as aggressive.

Practise varying the volume of your voice so you get a sense of the full range you have available.

The voice of uncertainty

When **people are nervous** they often speak in a **hesitant, jerky, uneven way**, sometimes punctuated with unnecessary pauses. Anxiety leads us to tighten up and stop breathing properly. This can make the voice sound high or shrill (especially in women) and swallowed or monotonous.

But although the **voice signals a problem**, it's not the **cause of the problem** – in the same way that the oil warning light in a car indicates a problem in the engine.

So the secret is to calm your nerves. You will also, typically, find it easier if you slow down and give yourself time to think.

What to do if your voice trails off

Non-assertive voices sometimes trail away at the end of sentences. Sometimes people develop a habit of speaking in this way. The problem can increase when they're feeling nervous. Follow these three steps to preventing a trailing voice:

1. **Be aware** This is the first step to fixing the problem.
2. **Be concise** Use short sentences so that you don't run out of breath.
3. **Breathe deeply** That way you'll have enough air to complete each sentence.

CASE STUDY

Sarah's boss asked her to represent her at a meeting with the senior team. She was aware that her voice can trail off, so she focused on her breathing and speaking in short sentences. This made her sound more in control and she was able to get her point across effectively.

Bullet Guide: Assert Yourself

End your sentences assertively

The inflection of your voice at the end of a sentence has a huge impact on how assertive you sound.

When your voice rises at the end – **a question inflection** – you come across as if you're not sure of yourself.

When your voice neither rises nor falls at the end – the tone is the same – it's a **statement**, which is firm but lacks power.

When your voice drops at the end – **a command inflection** – you speak with authority and assertiveness. Leaders often speak this way naturally. If you want people to act on what you say, consider dropping your voice at the end of a sentence.

Command

Um, er …

Using fillers such as 'er' or 'um' in everyday conversation lets others know that **you have more to say** – which makes conversations flow well. But use them excessively and you will sound uncertain – in which case you need to reduce them.

Do
- ✔ *Pause between sentences.*
- ✔ *Breathe during the gap.*
- ✔ *If you speak quickly, slow down.*

Don't
- ✘ *Focus on your filler.*
- ✘ *Forget to breathe.*
- ✘ *Speak quickly.*

CASE STUDY

Tom was in the habit of saying 'basically' and 'okay' a lot when he spoke, both formally and informally, and it soon became a **running joke** in the office. He sounded clumsy and that affected his ability to assertively influence others.

Bullet Guide: Assert Yourself

What do I do if my voice sounds aggressive?

Most people behave aggressively from time to time. Minimizing this tendency leads to better relationships.

Ask yourself, does my voice have any of the following qualities?

- very firm, steely quiet or harsh and loud
- sarcastic tone
- abrupt or clipped
- hard, sharp, precise and measured
- strident, maybe shouting or dictatorial.

If you suspect that you sound aggressive at times, you'll need to **lower the volume, soften your voice** and add some **warmth** to your tone.

We often refuse to accept an idea merely because the tone of voice in which it has been expressed is unsympathetic to us.

Friedrich Nietzsche

5 Power talk – the language of assertiveness

All too often people don't express their feelings, opinions, wants and needs as assertively as they might because they use **words and expressions that are weak and wishy-washy**. But it's easy to **turn your language around** and make your statements **powerful, strong and assertive**. This is particularly important in an age where **so much communication is via email**, and voice and body language don't play a part.

But words are more powerful than anything.

Jennifer Donnelly

This chapter will help you to:

* say what you mean in a direct and assertive way
* avoid sounding non-assertive by using powerful language
* get results by being specific and nailing things down
* understand the difference between questions and statements
* stop littering your language with self-effacing comments
* harness the power of 'I' statements
* become more assertive by using direct language.

Saying what you mean, meaning what you say

Many people don't clearly say or write what they mean. Instead of saying things straight they're vague and apologetic. This may be because they've got into the **habit of making things more palatable** for others at the expense of getting across clearly what they want.

One way of describing this is wimp talk vs power talk. Wimp talk is weak, wishy-washy and relatively non-assertive. Power talk is short, specific, clear, direct and much more assertive.

Wimp talk	Power talk
Indirect	Direct
Uncertain	Certain
Vague	Specific
Open ended	Nailed down
Questions	Statements
Apologetic	Confident
Self-effacing	Self-assured

Be direct

All too often people 'hint', 'suggest' and 'propose' instead of saying clearly and directly what they want. When you're assertive you're far more likely to get the outcome you want.

Indirect communication 'The bathroom is looking tatty.'

Direct communication 'You need to decorate the bathroom.'

Indirect communication 'It would be useful if you could get those figures ready.'

Direct communication 'I need the figures by 4 pm today.'

Indirect communication 'We should think about going on holiday.'

Direct communication 'I want to go on holiday.'

Uncertain vs certain

Sometimes **people express themselves** in ways that make it **sound as if they're uncertain**. They use words such as 'hopefully', 'maybe' and 'possibly'.

For example, 'I was thinking this is maybe the best way forward.' Assertive alternatives would be 'I think this is the right course of action' (quietly assertive) or 'This is the right course of action' (firmly assertive).

There are, of course, **situations** in which you want to make it plain that **you're offering an opinion and are inviting others to do the same**. 'I think this is a possible course of action. What do you think?' But don't make a habit of qualifying everything with 'I think' or 'I believe'.

> **Happiness is when what you think, what you say, and what you do are in harmony.**
>
> Mohandas Gandhi

Bullet Guide: Assert Yourself

Be specific and nail it down

Which of the following is more likely to achieve the result you want?

1 Can you send me the sales figures ASAP?
2 Please send me the sales figures by 9 am tomorrow.

It's not difficult, is it? The answer is 2. If you ask someone to complete something as soon as possible, don't expect to be at the top of their 'to do' list. **Specifying a date and time is assertive and effective.**

CASE STUDY

Lucy asked Tom to provide research data for the marketing plan by 4 pm on Monday. Tom looked at the rest of his 'to do' list and decided that he needed to prioritize getting the data done in order to meet her deadline.

Questions vs statements

If you want to be assertive, you need to take care with **stating opinions as questions**, which a surprising number of people do. Let's take a simple example. You want lunch at one o'clock.

Non-assertive Would it be useful to have lunch at 1 pm?

Assertive I'd like to have lunch at 1 pm.

While questions are a valuable part of communication, some people use them habitually **to avoid putting forward their opinion too strongly**. If this is true of you, make a **shift towards using statements and you will sound more assertive**.

Self-effacing vs self-assured

Ask yourself

'I don't know much about this but …' or
'I'm no expert …'

Do you ever start sharing your expertise in this self-effacing way? If the answer is yes, **you're immediately diluting the power and impact** of whatever you're about to say next.

Some people habitually use self-effacing expressions such as these. If that's you, plan to break the habit. Start, instead, by offering opinions without feeling that you need to qualify them or add caveats – and notice how many more of your ideas are taken on board. Keep doing this and you will quickly replace the old habit with a new behaviour.

Use 'I' statements

Using 'I' rather than 'you' in a statement is often more assertive and means you take ownership for your feelings. It's best to avoid 'you' language because it blames others and produces a defensive response.

Use	Avoid
I feel …	You make me feel …
I think …	You think …
I want …	You should …
I prefer …	Don't you think …
This is important to me …	It's your fault …

Take care not to use 'I' statements in a way that means that they still express an opinion or judgement, for example 'I feel that …'. Instead say 'I feel upset/frustrated/sad/angry when …'

Top tips for making your language more assertive

1. Review your emails before you send them and change the wimp talk into power talk.
2. When preparing to **present your ideas** at a meeting plan the content to **include power talk.**
3. **Practise using assertive language** whenever you make a request or offer an opinion. Then extend it to every area of communication.
4. **Ask someone you trust for feedback** on what you can do to make your language more assertive.
5. **Record yourself** speaking and consider how you can say what you want, think and feel more directly.

6 Saying what you think, feel and want

It's a fact: **saying what you think and feel** is central to assertiveness. This can be a real challenge for many people who hold back for fear of damaging their relationship with other people. Once you are aware of what to do it is easier than you might think. Whether you want to be able to offer opinions with ease or **make requests that people act upon**, what you need is a **handful of techniques** that assertive people use. The next step is to practise using them to **achieve success in a variety of situations**.

This chapter will help you to:

* offer opinions without feeling uncomfortable
* make requests assertively and get more of what you want
* achieve a mutually workable compromise
* use the broken record technique rather than giving in too easily
* use empathy when making requests to accelerate your rate of success
* follow up on requests effectively
* escalate your request to someone who has the authority to help you.

How to offer opinions assertively

Not everyone is comfortable **saying what they think or feel**. For some people it's like **sticking their head above a parapet**. When you 'put it out there', you might get 'shot down in flames'. Maybe it's better, they say to themselves, to **keep your mouth shut** and avoid the potential pain.

But if you don't say what you think or feel, **you can't influence what happens**.

Learning to speak out is a skill – and one that improves with practice. Start with 'safe' situations and people you feel comfortable with.

Avoid loud or challenging individuals at first – some family members or senior people at work can be among the most difficult to handle. You can **gradually build up to handling tough situations**. It helps initially to plan your remarks ahead of time.

You have an assertive right to have an opinion and to share it. Start saying what you think and feel, and you'll never look back.

How to make assertive requests

The secret of making assertive requests is to say, clearly and unambiguously, what you want. Be honest, direct and specific.

Assertive requests

'I like the house to be tidy. I would appreciate it if you would pick up your things.'
'Please empty the dishwasher before you go out.'
'I need the report by 10 am tomorrow.'
'I would like you to write the executive summary.'

The broken record technique

Most people give up too easily when others push back. The broken record technique **helps you stick with it**. It works like this: you **keep repeating your request** more times than you would naturally – **most people give up after two or three attempts**.

It's called the broken record technique because it's like an old vinyl record that gets stuck in a groove and plays the same line time and again.

Four steps to using this effective technique:

1 Succinctly express your wishes.
2 **Repeat it** until the person realizes that you mean what you say.
3 Go beyond your comfort zone.
4 **Keep going** until the person accepts what you say or compromises.

Bullet Guide: Assert Yourself

Dialogue like this **could go on for much longer** if needed:

James: 'I need the figures for the board report by 3 pm.'

Will: 'I'm busy. You'll have to do without them.'

James: 'I appreciate that you're busy and I need the figures by 3 pm.'

Will: 'I've got other important work to complete.'

James: 'I understand that you have important work, and I need the figures by 3 pm.'

Will: 'I can't complete your figures and get the wages done on time.'

James: 'I understand that the wages need to be done, and I need the figures by 3 pm to complete the report on time.'

Will: 'I guess I can do it if you get someone to help with the wages.'

James: 'That would be great. Can you ask Jo to help?'

Empathy – the oil in the engine

Without empathy, assertive techniques aren't always successful. You want to push without seeming pushy. Empathy is like the oil in an engine that keeps things working well. **Without it the other person doesn't feel heard**. This is especially important with the broken record technique.

When you express understanding of the other person's situation, **it softens your message**. But it's important not to take it too far and end up sounding non-assertive. All you need is to **acknowledge** what he or she has said or may be feeling.

Example

'I understand how difficult it is and how overworked you are at present [empathy] – **and** I still need you to complete it [assertion].'

It's important to **include the word 'and' rather than 'but'**. This is because 'but' negates what has gone before it and you won't sound genuine.

Going for a win–win situation

In *When I Say No I Feel Guilty* Manuel Smith says, 'Providing your self-respect is not in question you can assertively seek an alternative solution to the problem by **meeting the other person half-way**.' He calls this a **'mutually workable compromise'**. Your aim should be to achieve a win–win situation.

For example: 'I can't stay late but I could come in earlier tomorrow if that will help.'

How to follow up on requests assertively

Many people feel comfortable making an initial request. It's when they have to chase someone that they discover that they don't have a **mechanism** for **assertively following up**.

Do

✔ Plan what you will say and how to say it.
✔ Remember that **you have an assertive right** to follow up on a request.
✔ **Remain calm** and keep in mind that the person may not be resisting deliberately.
✔ **Get the balance right** and be strongly assertive.

Don't

✘ Plough ahead without thinking about how to express yourself.
✘ Worry about coming across as pushy.
✘ Let your frustration or other emotions leak out when you talk to the person.
✘ Go over the top – or you'll end up being aggressive.

Bullet Guide: Assert Yourself

Make things happen with escalation

When people don't respond to your request, **you can escalate by asking to speak to someone in a position of higher authority**. Many people, however, **find this aggressive**. A better solution is to tell the person you don't want to do that, but will have no choice if you can't find some way of solving the problem. This often works more effectively.

Refer to a higher authority

I don't want to get you into trouble by taking this higher – how can we resolve this between us?

⬆

Strongly assertive

I understand you have other things to do, and if I don't have your input now we won't complete the report on time

⬆

Firmly assertive

I appreciate you're busy, and I need your input for the report in the next 20 minutes

⬆

Quietly assertive

Please let me have your input for the report by 2 pm

7 Pushing back and saying 'no'

'No'. For many people this is the **hardest word to say**. They feel that by **refusing a request** they'll be thought **unhelpful, selfish and uncaring**. Even those people who think they can say 'no' easily, frequently find it tough in some situations such as with friends and family. But when you can't say 'no' you find yourself doing things you **don't want to do**. You have an **assertive right** to refuse – without feeling that you have to justify or explain. Saying 'no' gets **easier the more you do it**. And you soon realize that **all the fears you had** about what might happen when you did were just **mirages**.

This chapter will help you to:

* say 'no' rather than agree to something you don't want to do
* avoid justifying, explaining or defending when you refuse a request
* appreciate the value of replacing 'but' with 'and'
* know how to disagree with others assertively
* be able to manage interruptions effectively
* stand your ground by setting and defending boundaries.

Half of the troubles of this life can be traced to saying yes too quickly and not saying no soon enough.

Josh Billings

Being able to say 'no' is essential

If you can't say 'no', you'll end up saying 'yes' to everything. That means that you're not in control of your life. You do what others want – not what you want. If you often say 'yes' when you mean 'no', you need to consider what's driving this behaviour, challenge the beliefs behind it and do something different.

What stops us saying 'no'?

* fear of not being liked by others
* believing that we 'must' always say 'yes'
* making other people more important than ourselves
* needing the approval of others.

None of these is a valid reason for having to say 'yes' when you want to say 'no'.

Options for saying 'no'

Stall If saying 'yes' is a reflex action when someone makes a request, this tactic buys you time to gather your thoughts and be more assertive.

Example: 'Give me a few minutes to think about it.'

Pre-empt You see someone coming over to make a request, and you get your 'no' in before he or she asks.

Example: 'Oh, hello Jack. I hope you're not asking for anything, because this is a really bad time – I'm already up to my neck in work.'

Deflect Why you? Maybe someone else could say 'yes' this time – it doesn't always have to be you.

Example: 'Is there anyone else who could help?'

Negotiate You don't have to jump when someone else says 'jump' – unless it's your boss or someone in authority. An option is to negotiate the time-frame.

Example: 'I can't do it now, but I could do it tomorrow after lunch, if that's any good for you.'

Saying 'no' assertively

1   Don't justify or explain – but give a reason if you want to

Wrong: 'I would if I could, but it's just that I said I would help a friend with a project, and I don't want to let him down.'

Right: 'No, I can't stay late because I have a commitment.'

2   Keep it brief – saying too much weakens your impact

Wrong: 'Well, you know …'

Right: 'No, that's not something I want to do.'

3   Actually use the word 'no' – don't be ambiguous

Wrong: 'I'm really not sure I'm interested in your raffle tickets.'

Right: 'No, I don't want to buy any raffle tickets.'

Bullet Guide: Assert Yourself

4 Be polite – but make your 'no' clear and firm

Wrong: 'I'm really busy right now, so I'm not able to go out with you.'

Right: 'I appreciate the offer, but no, I don't want to go out with you.'

5 Don't apologize profusely – you have an assertive right to say no

Wrong: 'I'm really, really sorry. I'm very busy, and it would be hard for me to help you.'

Right: 'I'm sorry. I'm not able to help you – it's a no.'

Disagreeing assertively

We all have our opinions and often **perceive situations differently** from others. How do you **disagree** without being aggressive? And **keeping your opinion to yourself** is, of course, non-assertive. Try these tips:

Do

- ✔ *State your opinion clearly*, e.g. 'I see the situation differently ...'
- ✔ *Give reasons*, e.g. 'I don't agree because it's too expensive.'
- ✔ *Say what you agree with*, e.g. 'I agree that the plan is a good one, and for me the timing is wrong.'

Don't

- ✘ *Be vague or understate your view*, e.g. 'I'm not sure I agree with you.'
- ✘ *Simply attack the other person's opinion*, e.g. 'That's the stupidest thing I've ever heard.'
- ✘ *Be completely negative*, e.g. 'I totally disagree with what you are saying.'

Managing interruptions

You're trying to **get something done** – and **people keep interrupting you**. It's so frustrating, and it happens a lot. You lose focus and waste time. They may have things they want you to do. How do you **manage such interruptions assertively** without being rude?

Top tips for managing interruptions assertively

1 **'Now is not a good time'** Be clear. Be firm. Say 'Now is not a good time'. Make sure your tone of voice and body language indicate that your position is non-negotiable.
2 **'I can give you 3 minutes'** When you want to be open to approaches, but want to limit them, set a strict deadline at the beginning of the conversation.
3 **Put a 'sign' up** Have some mechanism for indicating that you are not available at that point.
4 **Say 'anyway'** If people outstay their welcome, use the word 'anyway' followed by a pause – which many people will realize means that you want to get on.

Setting and defending boundaries

Establishing boundaries and **standing your ground** is an essential element of healthy relationships at home and at work.

Do

✔ ***Take action*** *when people's behaviour violates your principles.*
✔ *Be honest and express how you feel about their behaviour.*
✔ *Describe **the behaviour you expect**, and ask them to honour it.*
✔ ***Manage the boundary** – point out lapses in the agreed behaviour.*
✔ ***Reinforce the boundary** as needed by reminding them of the agreement.*

Don't

✘ *Accept other people's poor behaviour and hope that it will go away.*
✘ *Soften the message in an attempt to avoid hurting their feelings.*
✘ *Be vague about what you expect from them.*
✘ *Think that it's enough to say what you want once.*
✘ *Let one incident pass by without drawing it to their attention.*
✘ *Give up – keep on reminding them until the boundary is no longer violated.*

Bullet Guide: Assert Yourself

Here's an example of language to use to establish, manage and reinforce boundaries:

Setting a boundary 'When you don't clear up your stuff I feel unhappy because the place is untidy. What I want in future is that we share equal responsibility for keeping it looking good.'

Reinforcing a boundary 'You agreed to share responsibility for keeping the place tidy. This week you cleared your things away for the first few days and by Thursday the place was a mess again. Please honour our agreement.'

> **Never allow a person to tell you no who doesn't have the power to say yes.**
> Eleanor Roosevelt

8 Feedback and criticism

How do you feel when you have to give someone negative feedback? Do you feel uncomfortable? Do you sometimes avoid saying what you really think? Do you 'sugar coat' it? What about when someone gives feedback to you? Do you feel defensive? Do you try not to take it personally and fail miserably? You're not alone if you feel this way. Many people don't enjoy giving or receiving negative feedback. And some people don't mind it at all. They see feedback as a valuable gift. Read on to discover how to give and respond to feedback.

This chapter will help you to:

* appreciate why feedback is an essential and valuable skill
* give great assertive feedback every time
* use the three Fs model for effective feedback that gets results
* take criticism in your stride and respond confidently
* give and receive praise assertively.

> **We are injured and hurt emotionally, not so much by other people or what they say and don't say, but by our own attitude and our own response.**
>
> Maxwell Maltz

Why is giving and receiving feedback an essential life and business skill?

1 Learning about what you do well **makes you feel appreciated**.
2 Specific positive feedback helps you **repeat more of the same behaviour**.
3 Negative feedback draws your attention to things to change.
4 You learn new and better ways of doing things and improve your performance.
5 By finding out what works, and what doesn't, you **build better relationships** with people.
6 Feedback helps you to **grow as a person**.

Bullet Guide: Assert Yourself

TOP TIPS FOR GIVING ASSERTIVE FEEDBACK

Be specific Give examples of what the person did or said.
Keep it simple Too much detail is overwhelming and undermining.
Be objective Not based on opinion but founded on firm evidence.
Make it balanced Acknowledge what was good rather than glossing over it.
Be honest Don't 'sugar coat' it or use wheedle words.
Focus on the behaviour – not on the person.
Be sensitive Think what it will be like to receive it.
Make it practical What can they do to change things?
Be supportive Let the person know that you care about their development.
Accept people They're doing the best they can – don't judge them.

The three Fs – fact, feeling, future

The three steps to giving effective and assertive feedback are:

| 1 FACT | 2 FEELINGS | 3 FUTURE |

1 **Begin by stating a fact**, such as something another person does, or describing something that happened.
2 State how you feel about that and explain the impact on you and others.
3 Conclude by saying what you would like to happen in the future.

There's no such thing as failure, only feedback

The following are examples of how this works:

Fact 'When you copy me on every email you send out …'

Feeling '… **I feel stressed** because it adds to my workload to read them, and then I realize I don't need them at all.'

Future '**What I'd appreciate is if you could** take a second to consider how important an email is before copying me in. Then I'll know that I do need to read it, and I won't feel unhappy about it.'

Fact 'When you arrived late for the meeting …'

Feeling '… I felt embarrassed and the client was kept waiting.'

Future '**What I'd like you to do in the future** is to plan things so that you arrive in plenty of time.'

Negative feedback – good and bad

CASE STUDY: BAD FEEDBACK

When Jo gave Martin feedback she knew that **he would challenge her**, so she **was careful** what she said. **She hinted** at what went wrong and implied what needed to change and was disappointed and frustrated when **his behaviour didn't alter**.

CASE STUDY: GOOD FEEDBACK

Sonia **explained to Beth that invoicing mistakes were having a negative effect** on the business, and after discussing the situation they agreed that Beth's **behaviour needed to change** to ensure that invoices were sent out on time.

Taking criticism in your stride

If you don't handle criticism well, it's likely that you will experience it as a personal attack. Those **who do respond well experience it in a detached way** – separate from them as a person. This is true even when the person delivers it badly.

To respond assertively to negative feedback:

* **Listen carefully** to what the feedback giver has to say.
* Thank the giver and ask for more information if you're not clear.
* Ask what specifically he or she was unhappy with.
* If the criticism is valid thank him or her, **agree and apologize** if this is appropriate.
* If it is not, thank him or her and **disagree with the parts that are incorrect** in a positive way.

Fogging

Use this effective and empowering technique and leave people who criticize unfairly with nowhere to go. **Stay calm and agree with only the aspects you feel have merit**. Use words or phrases such as 'I agree …', 'It's true that …' or 'You're right that …' and follow this with only the part you agree with.

If someone says 'You're always making mistakes!', you calmly respond 'I agree that sometimes I do make mistakes.'

By **agreeing with what is true** and **denying what isn't**, you prevent the other person from intimidating you or putting you down.

Negative enquiry

This technique is **great for encouraging honest feedback** and **dealing with manipulative behaviour** and 'put-downs'. By calmly asking for more specific criticism you encourage constructive feedback.

If someone says 'You're so untidy!', you calmly respond 'In what specific ways do you think I'm untidy?'

Giving and receiving praise assertively

Giving praise assertively

- ✔ *Maintain eye contact.*
- ✔ *Make it specific so it can be replicated.*
- ✔ *Be clear and brief.*

Example: 'I like the way you handled the team meeting and managed to keep to time.'

Receiving praise

- ✔ *Thank the praise giver briefly.*
- ✔ *Agree with or accept the praise.*
- ✔ *If you disagree, thank him or her and qualify your response.*

Example: 'Thank you, Jatinder. I was really pleased with the report.'

9 Assertiveness in challenging situations

Some people find it easy to be assertive in everyday situations but struggle when faced with difficult people or in specific environments such as meetings or interviews. What do you do when there are lots of people with strong opinions arguing their case? Or if it's a fast-moving discussion and you don't have enough time to think through fully what you're going to say? On occasions when your assertiveness skills really get tested, you need to stay calm and keep your insecurities under control.

When we long for life without difficulties, remind us that oaks grow strong in contrary winds and diamonds are made under pressure.

Peter Marshall

This chapter will help you to:

- deal more assertively with forceful characters
- respond more resourcefully to put-downs
- handle senior people more confidently
- learn to speak up assertively in meetings
- sort things out when you get bad service
- assertively manage family and friends better.

Handling forceful characters

Many of those who want to be more assertive struggle when faced with forceful, dominating characters.

Sometimes aggressive, usually intimidating and often abrasive, they can all too easily **trigger any insecurities** that someone who is quieter and conflict averse might have. Such people typically have a **'my way or the highway'** attitude and don't shy away from a fight – in fact, they often go looking for one.

How do you deal with such people? Like this:

1. **Don't take it personally** It's not about you – it's about them. They treat everyone the same.
2. **Keep your emotions in check** Their behaviour can feel like a dagger through your heart, but you need to remain detached emotionally if you're to deal with them.
3. **Don't retaliate** If you rise to the bait and get aggressive, or shrink to accommodation or avoidance, they've won. Stay calm, and be assertive.
4. **Be comfortable with conflict** You may not enjoy conflict or confrontation, but you need to be okay with it.
5. **Stand your ground** Forceful characters don't give up easily, so you will need to learn to be resolute yourself.

Right, boss – here's what I think

Many people find it hard to **handle senior people** assertively. Why? Because they have the **power** to reward and punish.

But that **doesn't mean that you have to be timid and meek**. You have an assertive right to raise issues with your boss, and **he or she has a responsibility to listen** to them.

Be clear what you want to say. Arrange a meeting. And **take your courage in your hands**. Any fears are likely to be unfounded. And even if you don't get the answer you wanted, you have at least tried.

Ask yourself
If you were a senior person – and maybe you are – would you want people to **speak up or sit quietly**? You need to know what your staff think, and **most bosses welcome open and honest communication** when it's done in a positive spirit.

Bullet Guide: Assert Yourself

'That's not our policy'

Ever tried to take something faulty back to a shop or deal with an official and been faced by a 'jobsworth' – someone who **invokes all sorts of rules** – often some variant of 'that's not our policy'?

Such people are not easy to deal with. They're often totally inflexible. So what can you do?

* Ask to **speak with the boss**, who may have more discretion, and be open to discussion.
* Use the broken record technique (see page 66), repeating several times what you want.
* Invite them to behave in alignment with a stated policy or principle. 'Your literature/advertising says you treat all customers fairly – how is this situation an example of that?'

Assertiveness in meetings

Many people find it hard to be assertive in meetings. This is particularly true when:

* There are many people attending.
* The subject being discussed is unfamiliar.
* Senior/important people are present.
* Some people are loud, extrovert and challenging.

Seven tips for being assertive in meetings

1 Prepare, prepare, prepare:
   a Read the agenda.
   b Decide what you want to say.
   c Make notes if necessary.
   d Be ready to share your thoughts.
2 Get to the meeting promptly – this has a number of benefits:
   a You can get settled and comfortable.
   b You can get a good seat facing the chairperson.
   c You can chat to people and break the ice.

3 Demonstrate assertiveness immediately:
   a Speak as soon as you can.
   b Don't wait to be asked.
4 Speak loudly and clearly:
   a Project your voice.
   b Enunciate your words.
5 Put your ideas forward confidently:
   a Speak with conviction and passion.
   b Avoid qualifiers such as 'maybe' or 'I think'.
6 Stand your ground when challenged:
   a When others disagree, restate your opinion.
   b Don't take objection to be rejection.
   c Remember it's not personal.
   d Don't get defensive and feel a need to justify.
7 Use assertive body language:
   a Lean forward to show engagement.
   b Gesture with your hands.
   c Make good eye contact with others.

Responding to put-downs and sarcasm

Aggressive people sometimes have **a patronizing and condescending manner**. They will use **sarcasm and put-downs** to score points and demonstrate their **superiority**. The secret is to respond assertively to the core of the communication and ignore the put-down.

Put-down	Response
'You're not very experienced in this area, are you?'	'I have lots of experience – and there are still things I need to learn.'
'That was a ridiculous comment.'	'I'm happy with what I said.'
'You're doing that report far too slowly.'	'I'm doing it carefully to avoid mistakes.'

Dealing with manipulators

Sad to say, but **some people do set out to take advantage of others** through manipulation and other techniques. There is also another, more subtle, and sometimes 'invisible', form of manipulation.

They might, for instance, say, 'You're great with PowerPoint – could you give me a hand?'

The most important thing is to recognize the request or comment for what it is – and not respond to it as if it's genuine. This frees you up to resist it, using any (or all!) of the techniques in this book.

10 Moving to being more assertive

Moving to be more assertive can **be scary**. Maybe you've **spent most of your life** up to this point **not saying what you think, want or feel** – and **now you're changing**. But what if it doesn't work? What if people don't like you? **What if …?**

Don't worry. That **won't happen**. Trust us. But you may want to take the development of your assertiveness skills **one step at a time**. Evolution, not revolution. That way **you'll feel more comfortable** as you move forward.

Bullet Guide: Assert Yourself

This chapter will help you to:

* move your assertiveness forwards in a safe way
* anticipate 'bumps along the way' and deal with them
* prepare a 'script' for more challenging situations
* create a mechanism for getting feedback from others
* go forwards into your future with confidence.

Even the longest journey begins with a single step.
Zen proverb

Simple and safe first steps

Here are some simple and safe ways of **starting to develop your assertiveness** skills – **in the order** we suggest that you apply them.

1 People you don't know outside work

When you have only **a passing transaction** with someone, and will probably **never see them again**, there's little or **no risk** in being assertive. That's why it's a perfect place to start – saying what you think and getting what you want in **restaurants**, **shops** and **offices**, and when dealing with staff in call centres.

2 Family and friends

Next step Tell family and friends you're aiming to develop your assertiveness skills, and that you'll **sometimes be firmer** in the way you deal with them in the future. Ask them to **be encouraging** while you're learning.

3 Supportive people at work
Then what? Pick some people at work you have a good relationship with, and try out your skills with them. It **might even be your boss**, if he or she has **raised the issue of assertiveness** in an appraisal.

4 More generally – in safe situations
Once you've **got all that under your belt**, and have expanded your comfort zone in using assertiveness, you can look for other, safe, situations – such as dealing with customers, suppliers and colleagues you don't know as well.

Preparing a script beforehand

One simple way of developing the skills of assertiveness **without risk**, or **making sure you get it right** in a specific situation, is to **prepare a script** of what you want to say. If you're speaking to someone over the phone you can simply read it. If you're face to face you can either use it as notes or remember the 'story' you developed.

Seven steps to preparing a 'script'

1. **Be clear about your outcome** What precisely do you want the other person to know, think, feel or do as a result of the discussion?
2. **Jot down some initial thoughts** Don't worry about organizing them. Just capture the key issues on paper.
3. **Sequence your ideas** The order is up to you, but having a structure is essential.
4. **Read it through** Does it say what you want to say? Is anything missing?
5. **Anticipate any response** Think of it like a game of chess. Be prepared for different responses on the other person's part. How will you react?
6. **Role play it with a friend** Ask someone you trust to act out the scenario with you. Get feedback from him or her. What can you learn?
7. **Review your script in the light of your roleplay** Then, if it's a really important assertive conversation, role play it again.

Bumps along the way

It's the same when **you learn any new skill** – you have some **bumps along the way**. Don't let them trouble you. Expect to have **set-backs**. They're **natural and inevitable**. Here's how **you can deal with them**.

What can go wrong	What to do about it
You end up being aggressive not assertive	Say sorry and learn from the experience
You're not assertive enough	Be more assertive next time
You say the right things, but your body language and/or voice are weak	Make sure that your body language and voice support the message
You fall back into wimp talk	Remember to use power talk
You give up too easily	Persist and persevere!

Getting feedback from others

The only way to **know for sure** that you're **making progress** in being more assertive is to **get feedback** from others. Here's how to do that:

* Invite others to let you know when they observe you not being assertive. Ask for specifics about what you did and didn't do.
* **Ask colleagues at work to monitor your assertiveness** in situations such as meetings where some people struggle to say what they think.

Ask yourself

'Who is **most likely** to tell me the truth?' The feedback **won't be of any use** to you if people are simply nice. Honesty is more valuable.

He did it – so can you!

CASE STUDY

For most of his life, Tom had thought of himself as **quiet and shy**. He felt and acted like a doormat. He only ever **really spoke when he was spoken to**, said nothing in most meetings and was passed over several times for promotion. But he came to realize, from his own observation and via feedback from his boss, that his lack of assertiveness and proactivity was holding him back. So **he decided to change**.

Little by little, step by step, **he learned how to say what he thought** and what he wanted. And he was astonished by how quickly he developed the skills he desired.

An exciting new world of assertiveness awaits!

Becoming more assertive really will change your life. It may even transform it. You'll find yourself achieving things you only dreamt of in the past.

As you become more assertive, **you'll find it easier to influence others** – to get your way while respecting them and preserving the relationship.

All you have to do is **start – and then continue**. It's as simple as that.

Enjoy the journey – and the success it brings!

You can learn to be yourself and live the way you really want to live.

Wayne Dyer